*The Magic
of
Inner Silence*

The Magic of Inner Silence

How to Connect With Nature and Rediscover Your Joy of Life

Brigitte Novalis

Novalis Press

Copyright © 2016 Brigitte Novalis

The moral right of the author has been asserted.

All rights reserved.
No part of this publication may be reproduced, stored in a retrieval system, or transmitted, in any form or by any means, without the prior permission in writing of the publisher, nor be otherwise circulated in any form of binding or cover other than that in which it is published and without a similar condition including this condition being imposed on the subsequent purchaser.

Published by Novalis Press

Print ISBN 978-1-944870-19-5
Kindle ISBN 978-1-944870-20-1

Typesetting services by BOOKOW.COM

What a joy to have
shared my journey
with you,
my wonderful
children,

Bettina Hoeppner,
Susanne Hoeppner
and
Christian Hoeppner!

And thank you,
Torsten Zimmer,
for your valuable
artistic and
linguistic advise!

To meet everything and everyone through stillness instead of mental noise is the greatest gift you can offer to the universe.

I call it stillness, but it is a jewel with many facets: that stillness is also joy, and it is love.

- Eckhart Tolle

In the Beginning

Insects

Winter Storms

Rain

The Brook

Prince

The Sparrows' Innocence

Epilogue

About the Author

The Pictures and Their Artists

Brigitte Novalis

In the Beginning

Did you ever dream of a beautiful, bright life? Have your dreams come true? Do you now live this happy life?

Or has your life become lackluster?

There are times, when life becomes a routine, when day follows night and night follows day without us noticing much. Maybe we notice that we become more tired and bored as the years pass by.

Our world appears dull, less radiant. The river of life does not dance in a lively way, but moves sluggishly, like a stagnant creek.

If we're truly lucky, we open our eyes a bit wider one day and take a good, close look at ourselves. This happened to me one January morning.

Brigitte Novalis

My family had left the house in a whirl of energies and the house was quiet. As I cleaned one of the bathrooms I looked into the mirror. My face was pale, my eyes tired, the corners of my mouth droopy. "I am no longer a girl," I thought. "I am getting older. I have responsibilities." They can weigh heavily upon us all! My shoulders hung downward. Even my breathing seemed difficult. I sat down at the edge of the bathtub and realized that I felt profoundly sad. For a moment, I cried. I felt sadness wash over me because I was no longer young and lively. My life had become boring and was no longer heading to new excitement, or so I thought. I did not run or jump anymore. I only walked. Why, I wondered, are my feet so heavy?

I pulled off my slippers and looked at my feet. Then I playfully moved my toes, as children like to do.

Do I feel my feet? Do I feel my toes? Of course, I was able to feel my toes with my hand, but I could not feel my toes simply from the inside.

If I cannot feel my body, really feel it from the inside, then I am not really alive, I thought, but only a shadow of myself. I cried even more.

"I want to be alive again", I said to my image in the mirror. "What can I do to be alive?" This thought seemed to wake me up. I felt brighter and almost energetic as if I had found direction again, a path to follow.

I washed my face and walked barefoot through the house. I felt the cold smooth tiles in the bathroom under my feet and the rough tiles in the hall. I felt the grained surface of the parquet floor, the woolen oriental rugs in the living room, and the soft carpets in the bedrooms. My feet felt, and I felt my feet. That was the day I started to feel my body again.

If you push open the door to yourself, you discover more and more. I noticed how my thoughts were running all around like hamsters in their wheels.

And my thoughts were so sad and resigned. So many 'should nots' and 'could nots'. How often had I seen spring, summer, fall, and winter. How many sunrises and sunsets had I seen! "Oh, I know that already, that is nothing special." When I saw the sun rising nowadays, I did not see the sun rise on that particular day in that one moment, but I saw all the sunrises and sunsets of the past, trivial experiences.

Memories were covering my experiences like thick layers of dust. I was buried under all the experiences of the past.

I knew then that I wanted more. I wanted to live, really live. So I started spring-cleaning within myself on that dark January morning.

I sat down on a chair, my feet flat on the floor, my hands on my knees. I gazed at the carpet two steps ahead of me and thought of nothing. Actually, in the beginning I thought a lot of things.

It is incredible how active the mind can be, how thoughts flow constantly, in rapid succession - thought after thought, image after image. I tried hard to quiet my mind, and began to sweat under the strain of it but I continued with my daily meditations for several days.

Then, in a moment of bliss, I found inner peace. After that, I found it easier to find this inner peace.

Over the following weeks it became easier to gently push aside disrupting thoughts. The more I succeeded in finding these moments of inner peace, the lighter my heart became. I started to live again.

Sometime later, in spring I was walking Prince, our German shepherd dog, in the woods.

The Magic of Inner Silence

Prince was sniffing at the scents of partridges or rabbits long gone, and once in a while raising his leg to mark a particularly interesting spot. I tried to breathe deeply and calmly and not to think of anything. For quite some time now, I had practiced meditating while sitting. Now, I wanted to meditate while walking; simply walking, looking, listening, feeling, breathing and being.

Again and again, thoughts and images came to mind. Again and again I gently pushed them aside; only walking and looking and feeling and breathing and being aware; gently pushing all other thoughts aside; only walking and looking and listening and feeling and being aware; only walking... being ....

Slowly and gradually I felt different. Something outside or inside of me was changing. The brook that meandered through the woods was flowing faster; it seemed to flow in my direction. Its water was lighter, clearer, and more crystalline.

Why did the brook appear so different? The thought almost stirred me out of my state of being. "Don't think," I gently nudged myself back, and continued to just walk and look and feel and be.

Then I did not **think** the brook was different, I **felt** it. I felt that the brook somehow had consciousness. It seemed to be as alive as the trees around me, as alive as the German shepherd playing at my side, as alive as I was.

There was no wind, yet the twigs of the trees were moving slightly as I walked by, as if they wanted to greet or touch me.

Even the songs of the birds were more meaningful than ever, as if they were singing specifically for me. "Don't think, just walk and breathe and feel and be."

Leaves and grass-blades were greener than I had ever seen them before, their greenness like shining jewels. A squirrel was running up a tree with incredible strength and grace.

This beauty, this splendor in all the life around me moved me deeply.

Joyful emotions flowed through me and I felt the loving presence of wonderful beings.

"What kind of wonderful beings?" I wondered.

While Prince started digging near a tree and I followed the winding path, I pondered what kind of beings were near, whose presence I felt. Could it be angels? Archangels? God Himself? Maybe those enlightened human beings who had walked this path on earth before us? Something like angelic friends? Wondrous beings?

When I stepped into the meadow, it seemed to be so fresh, so rich in flowers and grass blades and leaves and insects and birds, more complete than ever before. With all my senses and all my heart I looked at this rich and radiant life, and it seemed to look back at me, expectantly.

My eyes fell on a small weeping birch. It was the only being within all the radiance that looked miserable with its sparse leaves and drooping branches.

All around it, flowers and shrubs were growing abundantly, the brook at its side gurgled contentedly, birds were singing and the sun was shining. But the weeping birch seemed to let her almost naked twigs hang sadly, as if dejected. I felt a nudging as if I was

The Magic of Inner Silence

supposed to do something to help the birch tree. But what, and how?

"You should have grown in Findhorn," I thought, "there they work miracles on plants." I had just read a book about the Findhorn Gardens in Scotland, where they discovered that we influence plants with our thoughts and emotions.

If, for example, you have two equally strong and healthy potted plants on your windowsill and you care for them equally by giving them the same amount of water, fertilizer and light, but you are kind to one plant and tell it every day how magnificent and beautiful it is while you criticize the other by saying "look at you, how pathetic you are, you can't even manage a single blossom", the praised plant will flourish and the abused plant will wither away.

I had not done this experiment myself, because I couldn't bring myself to hurt my houseplants but I thought it was amazing that we could probably interact with plants.

All different kinds of information about trees came to my mind now as I stood in front of the weeping birch. I had read that trees have an aura around them, just like all living beings, their own energy field. I had read somewhere that if you sit on the ground and lean your back against the trunk of a tree, you can take in some of its life energy, which can heal and rejuvenate you. This memory triggered a thought. If human beings were able to take in some of the life energies of trees, then it should also be possible for human beings to give life energies to trees. The principle should work in both directions.

As I walked closer to the birch tree, I suddenly became aware of the absurdity of my thought. Heal a tree? Unheard of! But ... on the other hand, if one never tried out new things, one never learned. That's exactly how and why we repeat worn-out patterns, slowly dying of boredom.

I stopped two steps in front of the birch. "May I give you some energies?", I asked the tree. It trembled in the soft breeze. Was this a yes or a no?

"What's the matter with you today?" a part of me asked myself, "Do you really think it's healthy to talk to a tree? It's about time you came back down to earth." Another part of me, however, was joyfully moved and trusting.

I crouched down under the branches and twigs of the weeping birch and placed my hands around its trunk. I thought, "Take as much of my energy as you need," and waited. My hands around the trunk tingled. After a while I got the impression that I was surrounded by an electrical field that emanated from the birch. Or maybe this electrical field was emanating from me to the birch.

After a while the birch under my hands seemed to vibrate. Waves of fine energies seemed to go up and down the trunk. "Be calm, breathe, listen, be aware,"

I thought. Love was flooding from my heart through my arms and hands to the weeping birch.

When the children came home from school I told them that I had given energies to the small birch that looked sickly.

It was possible that nothing would come of it, that

my intuition was wrong. But if the birch did recover and grow more leaves, then the kids could learn right from the start that sharing energies with plants was possible.

I began to visit the small birch tree every day and placed my hands around its trunk. When I closed my eyes and became quiet, I could feel wavelike energy movements between me and the birch tree.

In the following weeks it grew more and more leaves. The foliage was not abundant, but the tree looked so much fresher. Finally, when after summer, fall and winter, the next spring came, the little birch tree was covered with leaves.

It was a seemingly simple step - becoming aware of my body and of my inner presence - that brought living awareness back into my body and into my thinking and feeling. As soon as I lived in my body and felt my inner presence, I could also feel the presence of those beings, whom I call wondrous beings. My wish for a beautiful, bright life was fulfilled.

Being Vibrantly Alive

If you want to live in the true sense of the word, you have to be at home in your body. Become aware of your body, enjoy being in your body and experience a new sense of being vibrantly alive.

Feeling Your Feet

Sit on a chair
and become aware of your feet
in your socks, in your shoes.

Become aware of the sensation
of your feet
resting on the floor.

Being at Home in Your Body

Walk barefoot on different floors
like wood,
tiles or carpets,
across garden paths and grass.

Allow your feet to experience
the different textures
and temperatures.

Feel your body from within.

Enjoy the sensation of being
at home in your body.

Brigitte Novalis

Insects

Many rainy weeks had passed since the healing of the birch tree. The rain poured down on the garden, the house, the meadow, the woods, the fields and on the birch tree, too. Eventually, the sun began to shine again, sparkling in all the raindrops on leaves and grass blades.

The children rushed out of the house and started playing with Prince, our German shepherd. He seemed to be relegated to the role of 'tournament horse' and jumping across their self-constructed fences. But he refused to jump unless they did the same, so all of them jumped.

The cats, which spent the rainy season moving from sofa to sofa and feeding bowl to feeding bowl, were also outside hunting for mice in the meadow.

Jan, a proud tomcat who seemed to believe that mouse hunting was beneath his dignity, lay in wait for water rats under the stone bridge.

I left the house and walked into the garden and through the meadow. The grass had grown abundantly and needed cutting. The nettles had grown miles long (or so it seemed!).

As I moved through the flowerbeds at the slope near the brook, pulling out nettles, the behavior of the birds attracted my attention.

Never before had they come so close. They fluttered around me nearly singing into my ears. They moved with me along the slope, accompanying me from

The Magic of Inner Silence

flower to flower, from shrub to shrub. I realized how much I liked them and enjoyed their songs.

"What a pity I cannot talk to them," I thought to myself. "Well, maybe I **can** talk with them, but would they understand me?"

As if in answer to my thought, a chickadee flew on to a branch in front of my head and bent down as if taking a closer look at me.

Then the front door was opened and the birds flew away. Later, they returned and again accompanied me through the garden.

In addition to the birds, we had many bees in our garden. They hummed around us in the flowerbeds, in the blossoming shrubs and the vegetable garden. We had been sowing borage for them because they especially liked the blue blossoms.

The bees visiting us in such large numbers were not the wild woodland variety. They belonged, instead, to a neighbor. Although he really loved them, his family did not share this dedication. His wife especially disliked them because she had been stung repeatedly.

"I don't understand why they sting you all the time, Mary," I said. "Your bees fly around our house, too, and they don't sting us."

"You live a quarter mile away from us," she replied, "and that makes a difference. You don't have as many flying around in the garden as we do." But they were humming and buzzing everywhere outside our house. I think the difference was, we had friendly thoughts for them. Since the children had been watching 'Maya the Bee' on TV, bees were among our favorite animals.

One day the children were cutting grass on the long meadow with the roaring lawn mower. My task was

to transport the cut grass by wheelbarrow to the compost heaps in the vegetable garden.

The borage plants to the left and right of the entrance into the vegetable garden had grown large, and it was necessary to push my way through them to get by.

Clouds of bees surrounded the borage plants. As I stopped in front of them with the full wheelbarrow, I had second thoughts.

So many hungry bees were humming around there, hundreds of them! "If they get upset and sting me, I will have to be rushed to the hospital," I thought. On the other hand, I knew that we wanted to live together in peace. For that, we all must make sacrifices. This included the bees, too.

I spoke directly to them. "Listen," I said, "we are happy that you like our flowers and we seeded the borage just for you to enjoy. But now I have to push the wheelbarrow back and forth through the borage. Have patience and don't sting me."

I pushed the wheelbarrow through the plants. Hundreds of bees were disturbed. A minute later I made the return trip; again, hundreds of bees were disturbed. Then I loaded the wheelbarrow, pushed it back across the stone bridge along the forecourt into the vegetable garden, and again I disturbed the bees. This continued for a full hour.

Nothing happened! Or should I say, much happened? Not one bee stung me. They seemed to understand my good intentions.

They seemed to have patience. All I needed to do was ask them. During those weeks and months I began to understand how polite animals are.

The Magic of Inner Silence

However, I didn't have as good a relationship with hornets. Far, far away in the woods, where the hornets would not bother me or my family, I accepted their right to exist, and wished them a good, peaceful life. But here in our garden, so near to us on every trip to the compost heaps? That was exactly where they liked to be.

One early spring morning they appeared. They did not come in large numbers, but whenever we emptied our kitchen bucket with vegetable cuttings, we always met one of them, a large, long, very warlike looking hornet.

When I was a child, I had heard some terrible stories

about hornets. I was told that if a person gets stung three times by hornets, that person will die. Supposedly, even a horse can be killed by only five hornet stings.

And these dangerous insects were now loitering at our compost heaps. Every day my children and their friends ran and played around the house and in the garden.

Would these hornets feel disturbed or threatened and sting them? Could these small children possibly die after a single sting? I could not let that happen. I had to confront the danger immediately. Next time, when I carried the kitchen bucket to the compost heap, I took a big shovel with me. When I saw a hornet rummaging around in the compost heap, I hit it. I hit it as forcefully as I could, again and again. I was cruel out of fear. At the same time I was very much ashamed of myself and in my mind I asked the hornets for forgiveness.

"But you have to understand that I have to protect the children," I thought.

"Do they really have to understand this?" I asked myself later. "Don't they also have a right to live?"

For several days I killed hornets, and I was ashamed. At night in my bed I would think about what I had done. Who could give me advice on this matter? Who could help me? The neighbors gave the advice, "Kill them but be careful not to be stung by them." That did not help me. Should I call the newspaper or the biological department of the university? Who else could I ask? Who was wise enough to give me good advice?

The wondrous beings came to my mind. Had I not asked them for advice before? Were they not my friends? So I asked them for advice. I sat down by the brook in the woods. "You wondrous beings," I said, "please help the hornets and me by giving me good advice."

I listened to the rustle of the leaves and the gurgling of the brook and calmed my mind. Then I listened inwards. I waited for something to happen, for something unusual to occur inside of me, a new thought or a new emotion as it had appeared with the birch tree. But nothing happened that day. I did get the answer eventually, though.

Several days later, when my husband returned from the office, he told me about an interesting radio program that he had listened to; it was a program about hornets and how precious they are as natural opponents of wasps.

The next morning, with two buckets filled with nettles, I went to the compost heaps, and watched two hornets so contentedly humming and eating around. I knew then that I would never again kill one. There had to be a better way. I stayed three steps away from them. With the bees I had reached an agreement. Why not with the hornets? Why did I not think of this in the first place? So I talked to the hornets.

At first I asked forgiveness for killing their family members. Then I explained that my only reason for doing so was to protect the children. I offered them a compromise. I asked them to fly away whenever we humans came to the compost heaps, and not to return until we left. I also told them that we were pleased that they could find good food in the compost and that we wished them well. The hornets continued to hum and rummage in the compost heap and did not seem to pay any attention to me.

My mind seemed to be "shaking its head". "Now you are really going crazy," it seemed to say, "sending energies to a little weeping birch, and appeasing some bees seemed strange enough, now you are making deals with hornets?"

My mind can be quite outspoken, but my emotions were peaceful. I slowly came to the realization that the time had come for humans to tread new paths. Resolutely I moved forward with my buckets. Both hornets flew up. They made small circles at first and then wider and wider ones above the compost heap until they flew away toward the woods.

And they kept to our agreement, every time. For three more years we lived in that home, and every time the hornets flew away in wider and wider circles when we approached the compost heaps. They did not sting us, and we did not kill them.

There was peace in our small world for a time until late spring, when the pea pods grew thick a plague came. Hundreds of small black bugs invaded our garden and set down on herbs and carrots, especially the peas.

Their numbers grew each day. They sat on the vegetables and herbs and gorged on our harvest. As they bred they grew larger and larger.

In the end, the older ones grew as large as small fingernails, and now we noticed that they were not just black but shining like mother-of-pearl. That was the only beautiful thing about them. Where they sat, as disgusting as black slime, plants wilted away.

I decided to remove all the plants that were invaded by the bugs to protect the non-invaded plants. I threw them into a deep hollow in the orchard, added paper and straw and then set everything on fire. I thought that a quick death in a split second would be the most humane way to get rid of these bugs. But it was all in vain. The next day we had even more bugs.

Our friends and neighbors did what they always did when nature proved to be difficult: they sprayed poison. "Eventually you, too, will learn to do so," they said. "Nowadays one cannot do without poison."

But poison was no alternative for us. We thought that we already had too much poison in the air, in the water and in the soil. But what else could we do?

The children, who had been watering the peas and weeding the garden for so many hours, were getting sad. All their work had been for naught.

"It'll be all right in the end," I told them. "One day the bugs will move on. After all, nature is friendly."

But the bugs did nothing to prove me right. Instead, their numbers grew. I pulled out more and more plants and burnt them with the bugs, but more and more plants were covered with bugs. Then the black bugs moved on to the beautiful flowers lining the vegetable beds.

Our neighbors were becoming bitter because of the time and effort required tending their vegetable gardens. A toxic war raged in their gardens.

Our garden, too, looked like a battlefield with the army of black bugs on all the plants. I realized that it was pointless to go on burning them. They seemed to breed even faster. But what could I do? Who could I ask who wouldn't recommend poison?

I stilled my mind and the answer came, of course, the wondrous beings! I went to our meadow, sat by the brook and listened. The trickling of the water and the rustling of the leaves calmed my mind even further.

"You wondrous beings, please give me some guidance. What can I do to prevent the bugs from devastating our garden?" No answer.

As I had done so often, I focused my attention inside my body; I felt my feet and legs, my hands and arms, my heart, gradually my entire body from within. I also became aware of subtle energy flows in my body. The more I became aware of these energy flows, the more distinctly I could feel them.

I played with these energy flows, lessened them by thinking of something else, and strengthened them by putting more attention on them.

I realized that my breathing became calmer and deeper.

Curious to find out more about the impact of my breathing, I breathed even calmer and deeper and after a while something unexpected happened. I felt light both within my body and surrounding it.

How long I stayed in this radiant inner light, I cannot say. After a while I became aware of still another light, a light neither dark nor bright. I can only describe it as a light beyond.

Beyond what? The known reality?

One of our cats felt these extraordinary energies. Flicka came and settled down on my knees, softly purring, and brought me back from wherever I had been.

However, intrigued by these experiences with the light, I played with the possibilities. I started to breathe in light, first through my nose into my lungs. That did not feel right. Then I imagined breathing in light through all the pores of my body and the energy seemed to follow my intention.

Breathing in light this way felt so good that I wondered if I had not been crippled all my adult life not having known how to breathe in light. These energy flows seemed to refresh every cell of my body. I felt vibrantly alive.

This time, when I asked the wondrous beings again, the answer came immediately, as an emotion. When put into words, the answer was simply:

"Talk to the bugs."

"What? I should talk to the bugs? To these ugly, disgusting pests?"

An emotion of regret flooded me, as if I had somehow failed. Were the wondrous beings disappointed with me? Then my mind received images in quick succession, images of us humans seen from far above. I looked at images of how we humans were multiplying boundlessly on this planet, of how we were spreading without consideration of other life forms. I saw us as similar to these ugly bugs. No, the bugs were not really ugly. Their repercussions were, though. And what of the repercussions of humans? In this world which we should peacefully share with other living beings, we don't act differently from these bugs. We pollute and poison our world.

As if in a time-lapse film I saw towns and cities growing rampantly into meadows and woods. I saw streets cutting mercilessly into woods and hills with their tentacles. I saw chimneys exhaling their poisonous breath. I saw pipes spitting poisonous water into brooks, rivers and lakes. I saw rubbish heaps spreading like ulcers on the living earth.

I wept. Oh, bugs, what a teaching! I have killed hundreds, thousands of you. Like a goddess of revenge, I interfered with your lives and burnt you mercilessly. I am ashamed for having burnt you. I am ashamed for having thought and talked contemptuously about you. Forgive me, forgive me.

After a while I went into the vegetable garden. There I talked to the bugs in thoughts and emotional images. "Please bugs, move on. Spread evenly on meadows and woods and heath lands. Leave our garden alone so that we can live here in peace. Please."

Within three days they were gone. The poisonous battle in our neighbors' gardens continued for two more weeks.

For a long time afterwards I still wondered why the bugs left our garden voluntarily. There was no deal between us. I did not make them an offer like: "Eat our peas but leave our beans alone."

I did not offer them anything except my apology and my compassion. The only thing I did was to ask them. That was all.

As it was my breathing in of light that deepened my connection with nature, I share my breathing meditation with you, dear reader. If you wish, you too, can breathe in light and over time become more receptive to the enlightening communication with the intelligent forces of nature.

Breathe Light – Be Light

An infinite ocean of
energy surrounds us.
When we breathe in light, we fill
ourselves with life energy. This energy
shines through all levels of our being and
into our environment.

Breathe slowly and deeply,
and as you inhale air into your nose
also breathe in white-golden light
through all the pores of your body.

As you exhale,
send this white-golden light
through your entire body
and eventually out through the pores
of your skin
into the energy fields
that surround you.

Winter Storms

It had been a cold winter. There was only a little snow and ice on the streets and walkways but still enough to make them slippery. We retired into the house where we enjoyed the open fire in the fireplace, around which we read aloud after lunch. Our pets kept us company - our dog lying at our feet, the cats curled up against us on sofas and armchairs. The long, dark, warm winter evenings seemed to be created for eating baked apples, drinking tea while talking, reading and telling stories.

In that winter I discovered Seth, an energy personality who was channeled by Jane Roberts. I was reading 'Seth Speaks,' 'The Nature of Personal Reality' and 'The Individual and Mass Events.' Seth taught me, showing me new ways of thinking that I had not found in years of studying philosophy at our university. Seth expanded my world view irrevocably,

opening up a world view where one creates one's own reality and where one lives in a matter-of-fact and meaningful relationship with the creatures and energies of nature. What I had experienced in summer, I served to my intellect to digest in winter. What a challenge for my intellect!

Then the storm came. It came from over the Atlantic, roared and surged across the Netherlands leaving a path of destruction behind. The TV showed blown-away roofs, whirled-away cars and snapped-off trees. Casualties were mourned. Now this storm was coming closer and closer to our area. Following the warnings on the TV as well the advice of our neighbors we carried bicycles and trash bins into the garage. The storm was getting stronger. We closed doors and shutters. I hardly managed to close the last rattling shutter at the storm side of the house.

With sorrow, I stopped in front of the large windows of our conservatory.

These windows had no gutters. If the storm snapped off a tree branch and it fell down on one of these defenseless windows, it would not only break the panes of glass but also the flowers and palm trees behind them. In my mind's eye I saw my beloved plants broken and crushed by glass splinters lying in a dark soup of soil, wood, glass and water on the tiles of the conservatory.

What could I do to protect them? While the storm was shaking me, I pondered how I could protect windows and plants. The storm was getting icier and wilder. It was really time to go inside.

At that moment Seth joined my thoughts. I remembered what he had said about weather in general and storms in particular. We are all interconnected with the powers of nature. Should I try to get into contact with the storm somehow?

"Not again," my intellect groaned. "Can you not let philosophy be philosophy and live a normal life like all the others? Hurry into the house or some of these branches might strike you down like the plants you are so worried about."

But there are times when I do not listen to my intellect. It does not always have the courage to move forward. I stood with my back to the house and looked into the direction of where the storm came from. Wildly it roared across Wanning's paddock toward our house. There were only a few shrubs, apple trees and pine trees between our house and the hissing breath of the storm. I tried to calm my thoughts and feel the storm.

Squalls shook me with greater and greater strength. To breathe, I held my arms in front of my face. In spite of my warm coat I trembled with cold. This storm was violent, powerful and wild. It pressed my body against the brick wall of our house like a stripped off-leaf. Even my thinking and feeling felt somehow pressed together. This power of nature was too powerful for me, too powerful but not hostile.

Before I ran into the house, I talked to my friends, the trees.

In my mind I sent them images and emotions. "Please protect our house. You are only a few trees but stick together. Splice the currents of air and let them glide across the roof. And please be careful with your branches. If you need to drop them, don't drop them into the windows of the conservatory."

While I said this in my mind, my intellect was moaning.

"Crazy, crazy. Who ever heard such nonsense?"

Later, inside the safety of our home, I was still icy-cold, so I took a hot bath staying long enough to get red like a boiled lobster. I drank several cups of hot tea. However, I was still shivering. Even later that night, lying in my warm bed, I felt some shivering in mind and body.

The storm was roaring like never before. Branches were breaking and falling down with muffled crashes.

Despite the uproar I was nearly asleep when I suddenly thought of the old elm tree in front of our house. The elm tree was about 250 years old. It towered above our house with its tree-long branches and could be seen for miles above the surrounding woods. Ivy plants as thick as arms entwined themselves around its trunk, a venerable tree.

But now I remembered what our neighbors had told us about it.

"You have to get rid of the tree," one of our neighbors had advised us, "if we have a really strong storm, it might fall on your roof and crush your beautiful house." - "Elm trees snap easily and tend to drop their branches. If it drops one of those heavy branches - then good night," said another. But not even in our dreams did we think of having it cut down. We loved the elm tree. It radiated peace and serenity. We felt snug under its branches.

On the night of the storm, however, I did not feel snug with its huge branches above our house. It was with melancholy that I thought that life always seems to ask us the question: "Your safety or my safety?"

Does it really have to be that way? Is it really unavoidable that we have to push someone back to have room for ourselves? Or have to cut down old trees to protect our houses? Is life really worth living if we can live in safety and peace only at the expense of others?

In Jane Roberts' books, Seth said again and again that we create our own reality. If so, I want to create my reality as I like it. My reality shall be a peaceful one. I decide to live in a world where each life is honored. A world of kind relationships between humans and animals and trees and other marvelous beings whom I can't even see or hear but whose presence I feel at times, like the wondrous beings. My thoughts quieted down. As I finally fell asleep, I had a thought in mind: "Please, elm tree, protect us."

The next morning I rushed into the girls' bedroom. "Thank God, the roof is not damaged." I opened the shutters and we looked out of the windows. The elm still had all its branches. There were branches and twigs everywhere on the ground, especially at the west side of the house.

A long branch was lying next to the house under the deep, large glass panes of our conservatory, but none of the glass panes were shattered. No roof tiles had been blown away. I thought, "thank you, trees."

Everywhere in the neighborhood the storm had caused damage. Our TV overflowed with damage reports and terrible news. Roofers, glaziers and car mechanics had a sudden boom.

We had two more storms that year, storms of a kind that Western Europe had not experienced in decades. Each time I talked to the trees. Each time we came through the storms without any damage.

At times, while standing under the huge elm tree, I wondered how during the storms, it could succeed in dropping only thin, small twigs while holding on to the big, heavy branches. One fine summer's day we went to see my parents. Only the cats stayed at home. It was a sunny day. A warm, soft wind was blowing. When we came home, a huge branch of the elm tree, as big as a tree, was lying right along the front of our house. I wondered: did the elm tree wait to drop one of its branches until we were all gone and safe?

During the following months I learned to clear my mind more and more. When I walked through our woods with Prince, I opened all my senses and my heart to the beauty and freshness of the flowers, bushes and trees around me.

My walk became a walking meditation. I felt a sense of gratitude for everything I felt and saw and heard in nature.

As I opened my inner senses to the energy-intelligence of trees, I became aware of them emanating gentle and caring energies for us human beings, like loyal shepherd dogs who watch over their people.

I felt then and still feel a great sense of gratitude for trees. Their beauty and gentle energies enrich our lives. Even more importantly, without trees we would not be able to breathe air. Without trees we would cease to exist.

To become aware of the beauty and the intelligent forces of nature, you have to become still. You have to open your senses to see, hear, smell and feel nature all around you. At the same time, you have to be present in your heart. This will take some practice but once you succeed, you are blessed with the magic of inner silence. You will see the deeper beauty of nature. You may even communicate with nature. By all means, your life becomes richer.

Brigitte Novalis

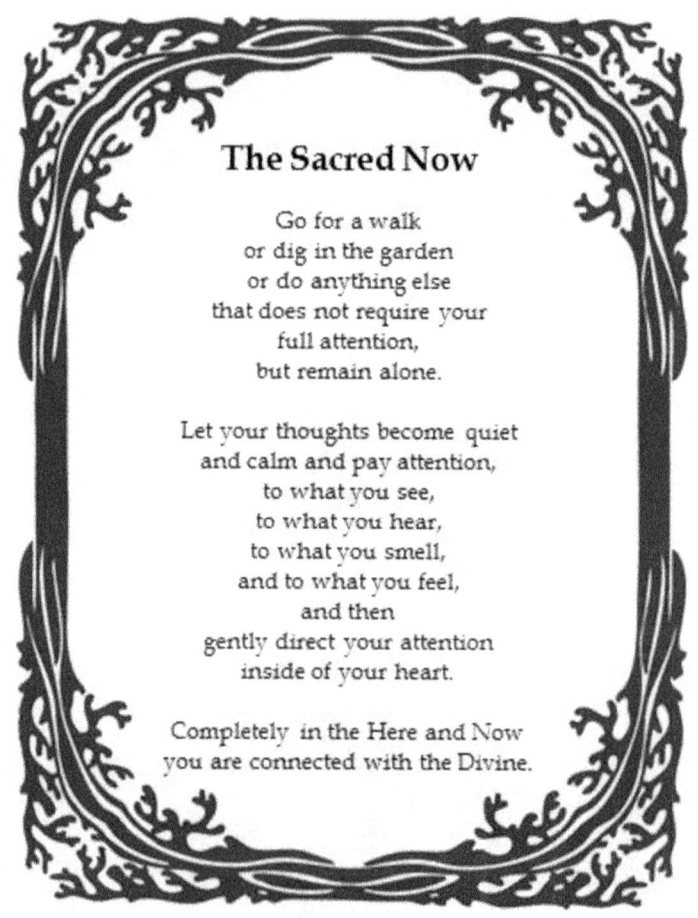

The Sacred Now

Go for a walk
or dig in the garden
or do anything else
that does not require your
full attention,
but remain alone.

Let your thoughts become quiet
and calm and pay attention,
to what you see,
to what you hear,
to what you smell,
and to what you feel,
and then
gently direct your attention
inside of your heart.

Completely in the Here and Now
you are connected with the Divine.

Rain

It was a warm, dry summer. For weeks the sun had been shining down from a cloudless sky. At first we were all happy. "Finally a really nice summer," a neighbor said. "Yes, this is a great summer, isn't it?"

People streamed into lakes and swimming pools. Ice cream was eaten by the bucketful. Tables and chairs were set up on sidewalks outside cafes. In the evenings the smoke from charcoal grills hung in the air. Finally a really warm summer. That's how it should be.

It stayed dry for several more weeks. The sun continued to shine week after week. Warmth turned to heat. Slowly people retreated from their hot back yards into their cool houses. They began to moan with frustration about watering the garden every day to keep flowers from withering.

After a while they complained even more because they were no longer allowed to water their gardens because water was getting scarce. The farmers saw a hay catastrophe approaching because the grass on the meadows was shriveling due to lack of rain. Now people did not talk about the really great summer, it became the summer of drought and heat.

Our children and their friends began to complain about the heat and drought.

"This is nothing," I said to them in our pleasantly cool house, the heat kept outside by its solid brick walls. "In Africa, in the Sahel Zone, where it is much hotter than here, it sometimes does not rain for seven or eight years. That's what I call a drought, no rain year in, year out. It was pretty hot for these people. Until one day, an old Indian lady came and brought rain."

"Brought rain? Really? How did she do that? Please, tell us."

I had discovered a very interesting book, Zeit ist eine Illusion (Time is an Illusion) by Chris Griscom. In one of its chapters she writes about the Hopi Indians, who live in the dry desert of Arizona. Dry desert or

The Magic of Inner Silence

not, they have cultivated maize there for more than four thousand years.

How is this possible? They know the art of calling the rain. Like other North American Indian tribes, one of their sayings is: "If your heart is pure, you will be able to call the rain."

To bring rain to some of the driest countries of Africa, Chris Griscom accompanied a wise woman elder of the Hopi tribe to Somalia. The old woman fasted and meditated for several days and then, watched by the elders of the villages around, she placed blue maize into the soil and performed ceremonies to call the rain.

And rain it did. It was not only a short shower. No. It rained for days, so generously that it got to be too much for the people there.

"And that really happened?" the children asked.

"Yes, that's cool, isn't it?"

Some years ago I had read some articles about it in the magazines and even seen some photos. At that time I asked myself, as many readers must have, 'Is this true or just a hoax?' As I read this book, however, and remembered the photos in the magazines, I thought that there must be some truth in it.

When you hear a story like this, the question arises as to whether an average person such as you or I is able to call the rain. The answer is yes. What is possible for one person should also be true for other persons.

But what of mass consciousness? If the population is undecided, say fifty-fifty, could a single person tilt the balance?

At breakfast we usually listened to the weather forecast for agriculture since we lived among farmers in the country.

One morning, as we listened again to the forecast for the whole week, they again predicted heat and cloudless skies for the week above Western Europe.

"Don't you want to take care of this and call some rain?" the children asked me hopefully before they took off to the bus station on their bicycles.

Should I? Do I have the right to interfere? Changing weather patterns and calling rain is a far-reaching matter. Besides, the responsibility is far too great. What an idea the kids had, just to provide for rain!

A while later I was biking through our neighborhood with Prince running at my side.

The meadows to the left and right had only short grass blades. The stems on the fields looked feeble. The ditches were dried-up.

The sky above me was not clear and transparent blue but more grayish blue, dull, as if there was a lot of water hanging high above in the sky. Could this be steam that did not want to turn into rain?

I stopped. Prince came over to my bike and looked up at me, expectantly.

I looked around. As far as I could see, there was no house, no stable, no tractor, no car, no bicycle besides my own, and no person to be seen.

I thought, should I try to call the rain? In spite of my having breakfast this morning? The Indian woman elder had been fasting for days. Well, with all these curious people around her, she probably wanted to make sure of a meditative state. I hoped that the fasting was not a prerequisite for the calling of rain. If it is our consciousness that has to be attuned with the consciousness of nature all around us, then such a small breakfast in the stomach couldn't be much of an obstacle, right?

How would I communicate with clouds, or with the steam in the air above? As I did with the weeping birch? Breathing slowly and deeply, quieting the mind and opening the heart? Asking and being grateful?

I imagined the steam above me turning into raindrops and splashing to the ground all around me. I imagined this as distinctly as I could. In my mind's eye I saw the whole sky above me at first filled with steam and then with raindrops that fell to the ground.

I created the sensation of having these raindrops all around me. I saw them fall, fall, fall down onto the dusty road, into the crevices of the dry clay soil, onto the brittle leafs, on roofs, on trees, on myself. I was already starting to feel cold and I expected a shower at any moment, at least a small, short one. Nothing happened. The sky appeared a little bit duller. That was all.

I turned and biked back. "Maybe it takes a special gift to call the rain, a special gift that only a few people have command of," I thought. "Or maybe it *is* necessary to fast to prepare for this task." Then I saw our neighbor Henry driving towards me, waving as he passed by. How lucky am I that he didn't come earlier and see me, standing with closed eyes, like a statue in the middle of the road.

At noon, when I had almost completed my cooking, I heard dripping and splashing outside. This could not be rain, could it? I rushed outside. Water dropped from the sky in heavy splashes - rain, which I had called.

Soon the rain stopped and the sun came back. The lawn was wet and the roof and the shrubs and the trees, as well as the kids who came biking home all excited.

Well, it was only a short shower. Hardly of any importance. Maybe an error of nature. The real proof that we humans are indeed connected to nature and can ask her to let it rain must bring lots of rain, masses of rain. One does not want to fool oneself.

Two weeks later I got proof. The weather forecast predicted another dry and hot week. I told the kids that I would again try to call the rain. I biked to the wheat fields. Afterwards we had two days of rain.

The Magic of Inner Silence

Now it is not my intention to suggest that you, dear reader, should call the rain or raise storms but to say that we do indeed have an influence on nature.

It is true what the enlightened masters of all times have told us. We are connected with nature. We are a part of nature. Invisible threads connect us with life all around us. We are not isolated, not alone, ever.

I was wondering what kind of threads these are that tie us together. What kind of feelers do we put out? And how? Is it not mysterious, simply magical, that we humans spin these mysterious threads that connect us with other people and with animals and plants and even with storms and clouds?

Web of Life I

Walk slowly in the
woods or on a
meadow.
Calm your thoughts.

Listen to the wind
playing
with the leaves.

Look at the shapes
and colors of leaves.

Smell the scent of
flowers, and of the
soil.

Sense the wind.
Feel the sunshine on
your skin and the
shadow.

Web of Life II

Are you aware of your
breath moving
through you?

Are you aware of the
pulsing of your blood?

Combine all
impressions and
become aware

of nature surrounding
you as a living
structure.

Feel how you are
embedded
in this structure.

You are a colorful
thread in the web of
life.

Brigitte Novalis

The Brook

In my search for the meaning of life I studied philosophy at our university for several years. After that, I learned to meditate and visualize. In the course of my studies, I also looked into Transcendental Meditation and Zen Buddhism.

I was truly fascinated by Zen Buddhism. For weeks, I contorted my bones to come close to the lotus position, as the masters teach it, or at least sit cross-legged during my meditations. However, these postures proved quite painful. Unlike our neighbors in Africa and Asia who sit on the floor with ease and grace, we in the Western world are brought up to rely on chairs and sofas.

Some fellow European meditators talked about 'befriending' this pain as a means of coping. They also spoke of ignoring the pain and killing the ego, a well-known concept in many spiritual traditions. While I heard their words, something inside me shunned these suggestions. With all due respect, I felt the time was here to walk new paths and deal with the ego in gentler ways. After all, it is part of our infinite consciousness.

As the years stretched through the circle of seasons, I learned about the magic of inner silence. I started by calming my mind and feeling my breath moving through my body, gently pushing away those thoughts that drift by on the surface of the mind. What to do and what to consider and do not forget that. I became more and more aware of my body, of the different temperatures of the air around it, of the clothes covering it, the texture of the floor beneath my feet.

As my mind became quieter, I became aware of my body itself - of its movements and energy flows, then finally of an inner presence within the body, a softly glowing, loving presence.

The more I was able to feel this inner presence, the richer and more colorful my life became. There was a greater clarity of perception, a new depth of emotion, a deep inner peace.

As I opened my heart and my senses more than ever before to the creatures and intelligent forces of nature, walls crumbled all around me.

Whether we are aware of it or not, our societies build solid thought structures around us. Our intellect is trained to function in well-established ways. Again and again we walk the beaten path. Forever we turn round and round. Fortunately, we can set ourselves free because we have been given free will.

As I listened to the voices of nature, my senses became more fine-tuned. My intellect also began to roam more freely. Over time, my intellect and intuition became friends. Whenever I 'forgot' the limitations in which our intellect 'has to move,' fascinating new ideas and pictures emerged in my mind.

The wondrous beings taught me step by step to reconcile the forces of my inner being. This was an important development; how can we live in harmony with others if we ourselves are scattered?

Zen Buddhism, especially as practiced in Tibet, fascinated me. One of the tools the Zen masters use to guide their students toward enlightenment is the 'koan,' a contradictory riddle of sorts – a paradox that cannot be solved by the intellect or the logical mind. From time to time the Zen master asks his student for the solution of the riddle. The student, who is devoted to his teacher and by all means wants to solve the problem, ponders it for days, weeks, or even months. He has this koan in mind whatever he does.

Then, one day, something unexpected happens to the student - a bang, a shock, maybe a fall, perhaps he breaks his leg. But this shock hurls him out of the usual way of thinking, and in a blessed moment he sees the world as it really is. This experience of enlightenment, as short as it might last, changes his worldview forever.

This is what I had to try myself: find a koan and then meditate.

Many well-known riddles came to my mind, for instance: "What comes first, the chicken or the egg?" or "What is the sound of one hand clapping?" But I wanted to find a koan for myself.

One day, walking through the woods by the brook with Prince, a question came to mind. "Is this brook

The Magic of Inner Silence

young because it rises in Henry's meadow next to our property? Or is it old because it has cut deep meanders through the woods since the last Ice Age?" That was a good koan, I thought. Best of all, it was one that I found myself. I kept this koan in mind as I was weeding, writing, cooking, feeding cats, meditating, studying, shopping and falling asleep.

One day, walking through the woods again, my mind filled with this question; and at the same time, very quiet, the wonder happened. My eyes were resting on the brook. I saw the brook, but it wasn't only a brook. It was a flowing being consisting of minute light particles.

These light particles flow not only within the bed but also high above it in the air. The brook is a joyful, powerful energy: thundering, overflowing, surging along, magnificent, overwhelming, and vibrantly alive. Yes, alive. This brook-energy has consciousness. I feel the joy within the brook-consciousness - power, enthusiasm, triumph. Something within myself answers to this. I myself am vibrantly alive, magnificent. The brook being, triumphantly aware of itself, and the Brigitte-being are rotating around each other, touching each other, dancing together. Joy, freedom, bliss .... understanding.

Then my mischievous intellect interfered. "Is this what they call an experience of awakening?" it asked, and the wonder vanished. Again the brook was just the brook. Again I was just Brigitte. The understanding slipped away. This door into another dimension slammed closed.

Back in the 17th century, the great mathematician and philosopher Leibniz made an interesting mind-experiment. "Imagine for a moment," he said, "that you have the sharpest knife of the world at hand, the thinnest scalpel to be imagined. With this knife you are cutting a piece of matter, such as a grain of sand, right through the middle - and then again and then again. You are cutting and cutting, and that grain of sand gets smaller and smaller. If you have been cutting for a long, long time – what remains? If you cannot cut anymore – what do you have in front of you?"

That is, more or less, what Leibniz asked. What do you think? What remains? What is the minutest unit of the grain of sand? Of every particle of matter? Leibniz called it the 'monad.' This most minute unit does not have height, depth, width, color, mass or weight. This entity is 'consciousness'.

Although that concept may at first seem difficult to understand, remember that at the beginning of the 20th century Einstein described the relationship between matter and energy with his famous formula

$$E = mc\text{ squared.}$$

Matter can be converted into energy, and energy into matter. Matter is akin to frozen energy.

We know from research done in quantum physics, that matter, at the level of atomic and subatomic particles, consists of pulsating energy fields. All matter, including our physical body, consists of vibrating wave patterns of energy. This fact has been known in ancient Chinese medicine and the Ayurvedic medicine of India for thousands of years.

It was known in ancient Greece, about 2,500 years ago, where Pythagoras said, "A stone is frozen music." It was a physicist of our times, David Bohm, who wrote, "A rock is frozen light."

David Bohm also wrote, "I would say that in my scientific and philosophical work, my main concern has been with understanding the nature of reality in general and of consciousness in particular as a coherent whole...."

It seems that the world around us is a pulsating field of aware energy, although our perception tells us otherwise. Trees and birds and rocks and clouds and the cells of your own body have their own frequency wave patterns of energy and awareness.

What I experienced with the brook in that special moment was the brook as energy/consciousness, that which lies behind this running water. I not only experienced the brook as energy-consciousness but myself also, and our energies were resonating.

The Magic of Inner Silence

For a brief instant the door into another dimension had opened for me. I experienced pure joy, pure bliss and understanding. The door slammed closed.

However, we all have the ability to open these doors. The activation key is a deep desire to be more aware and expanded. The basis to make this happen is the magic of inner silence.

Eternal River

Water cleanses and heals, but you don't need to actually swim in a pond or river in order to experience the healing power of water.

As you breathe slowly and deeply,
picture yourself next to a river.
Become aware of how
peacefully it flows
and how clean its water is.

Slowly step into the water
and feel how warm and refreshing it is
and how it carries away
fears and anger and doubt and pain.
Eventually you become as clear as the water.

Dive deep into the river, knowing that
you can breathe in the water
whenever you wish.

Prince

When the mind starts to reach out of its snail-shell of habits, the seemingly solid structure of our life starts moving. When we grant a larger scope to our wider, freer self, we may be carried forward by the stream of life as if by a huge surge. My family and I were carried forward by such a surge all the way from Germany to North America - Boston.

Our German shepherd, Prince, followed us faithfully as all loyal hearted dogs will. Prince was a beautiful dog, but when we saw him at the shelter so many years ago, so shy, so scared, we did not notice his beauty. However, we were touched by the way he looked at us.

During the first weeks in our house he resembled a crushed bundle of fur more than a stately dog. He hid behind chairs and crept into corners at every sound. He hardly dared to eat or drink. If one of us came close, he trembled all over.

As time passed, however, he seemed to stretch and grow as he learned to trust us. As he held his head higher, we could see that he was not only tall but also magnificent.

How life is enriched with such intelligent, loyal and sensitive friends at your side!

They are always ready to accompany you for a walk no matter the weather, always happy when you come home, and love you no matter how dreadful you feel or unfriendly you behave.

Dogs and cats are heart openers.

Prince moved to Boston with us into a well-furnished but dreary building, the walls of which seemed drenched with gloomy memories. The whole neighborhood appeared soaked in hopelessness. It was with a faint shudder that I walked up toward the house, darting through the dark stairwell into the door of our apartment.

Inside our rooms were bright, warm and friendly. Prince was there, waiting for me: I entered a different world.

Months later, Prince moved with us into a new bright house. He enjoyed life so much more now! He hiked the Blue Hills with us; strolling through the woods with us and retrieving sticks from ponds. He followed me through the house and watched my daughters do their homework. He waited for us. He was always there for us.

One day I noticed that his belly was swollen and that his movements had become quite clumsy. I brought him to our veterinarian. "That does not look good," he said. "Please drive him to the animal hospital to be x-rayed. I will call the hospital to let them know you are coming."

How sad and worried I was as I drove Prince to the animal hospital. When we entered the building, Prince looked at me anxiously. "Whatever the case,"

I told him, "I will take you home with me again. I only want to know what is wrong with you so that we can help you."

Prince waited patiently as I completed the necessary paperwork. An aide came with a blue nylon leash to bring him to an examination room. Again Prince looked at me anxiously. "Go with him," I told Prince. "I'll pick you up afterwards. I promise." Trustingly, he followed.

I drove home and walked around the house restlessly, waiting for the call from the hospital. A few hours later they called. "Your dog has terminal cancer of the liver," I heard an indifferent voice saying. "His belly is swollen because he has internal bleeding. You can just leave him here."

"What do you mean?" I asked.

"As there is no cure for him, and as he is here already we can put him to sleep right away. You don't need to come back. We will send you an invoice."

My heart began beating painfully. Do they expect people to desert their best friends when they are dying?

When I returned to the hospital to bring Prince home, Prince was led back into the hall by the aide. I stretched out my hands to him. He put his head into my hands.

We felt he knew these were his last days in this life. We had also made up our minds that we would put him to sleep as soon as we felt that he was in pain.

Those last days he walked very slowly but he still brought us his tennis ball, which he caught as elegantly as ever. He no longer slept downstairs in the house but beside my bed.

In that week I lived only for him. It was the week before Easter, and the girls rushed home from school as fast as they could. We wanted to spend every remaining hour with him.

One morning, as we prepared to leave for school, Prince followed us into the garage. To our surprise he slowly and arduously got into the car. When I came back home from dropping off the girls, he did not want to leave the car.

At first I thought that it was too difficult for him to get out of the car but then I noticed that he did not even try. He did not move when I called him to come. He just looked me in the eyes. Then I understood.

"Prince, do you want me to drive you to the vet? Has the time come?"

He briefly waved his tail. I started crying. "I will bring you to the vet when they open. Right now it is too early. Please, get out of the car for now."

He followed me slowly and with obvious pain. I left a message at the vet's. We were expected at 9:00 a.m. The dreaded day had come. We had to part. Prince was lying next to me on the carpet, panting. I patted him and cried. I wished I could have stopped time, but time went by relentlessly.

When we arrived at the doctor's office, Prince got out of the car willingly but with difficultly, and slowly walked to the small treatment room. He lay down, and I could feel how much he trusted us. As he looked me in the eyes I felt his love for me. The vet talked to him in a soft voice and prepared the injection.

Then he turned to me.

"You should take care of the paperwork first; afterwards you might not feel like doing it. We'll wait for you." He took Prince into his arms. When I opened the door to leave the room, Prince screamed. He screamed like a human being in utmost pain and despair. I ran back to him and took him in my arms.

"I am not going to abandon you in your last hour, Prince. After all, you are my beloved friend. I'll be back in a moment."

I signed the papers in the office. I could hardly read them through my tears. Then I went back and held Prince in my arms once more. I felt his last breaths and then - the silence.

I felt numb when I drove home. When I got home I could not bear to stay there. I drove to a comforting place, Infinity Books. I parked and stood waiting to cross the street. Tears were streaming down my face.

"Do you also cry, Prince?" I asked as I walked across the intersection. Immediately some large raindrops started to fall. I looked up. There were only some small white clouds at the blue sky. A woman walked toward me at the intersection from the opposite direction.

"Isn't this weird weather?" she said, "Mostly blue sky and yet rain!"

It continued to rain all the way to the bookstore. Even inside the store I could hear the rain pouring down.

"Is this really rain?" asked the young man at the desk. "Where is it coming from? The sun is shining and yet it rains. The weather becomes crazier every day."

I sat down on that blue leather sofa in the New-Age-corner with a couple of books, listening to the gentle music of 'Deep Forest' and breathing in the incense. But I could not bear to stay there either. Again I drove home.

How empty my home was! Oh, Prince, I thought, I miss you so. I lay down on my small sofa and cried.

"You wondrous beings," I said, "please show me Prince and let me know how he is doing. Please."

I closed my eyes and pictured Prince in front of me as I had seen him at the last time here in the house with his swollen, partly shaved belly. Soon this painful picture faded away and another picture emerged from my inner mind.

I saw Prince standing in front of me healthy and magnificent, waving his tail at me. He came closer and licked my hands. He was in a park with many other dogs that were running and jumping around happily. Some dogs ran past him as if to say: "Come, run with us."

And so he did. He ran after the other dogs then turned back to me. He looked me in the eyes with love and ran off again. They playfully chased each other. No doubt, Prince was doing fine.

He returned again with another beloved pet, our boxer dog. Both licked my hands, and then ran off with the other dogs.

They came back again, this time with a small dog that was vaguely familiar to me. Then I recognized him as the dog of my childhood. He also waved his tail at me. For so many years I had not thought of him, and now he was standing there with the other dogs.

How different they were - the dachshund who waved his thin tail so merrily, the boxer who waved his rear so effusively that his whole body shook, and the magnificent Prince with his elegant movements.

Again and again they came back to me to show me their love. Then the images faded away.

The girls rang the doorbell. One glance on my face told them that Prince was gone. He was still there but no more in his physical form.

Life without Prince was somehow rough and with sharp edges. The air seemed colder and the shadows darker

The Magic of Inner Silence

As I write down these experiences with Prince, I have tears in my eyes. I still miss him so. Suddenly a song comes to mind. I hum it. It is the beautiful Evita-Peron-song: "Don't Cry for Me, Argentina." Now I sing it loud. "Don't Cry for Me, Argentina." It seems funny that I sing although I am so sad, then I realize what I am singing: "Don't cry for me!"

Although I cannot stop crying, I say: "No, I don't want to cry for you anymore. I understand. I won't cry for you." And again this song comes so strongly to mind. I cannot help singing it again.

Now it is another line that stands out: "The truth is, I've never left you." You have never left me, Prince? You are somehow still there for me, for us? I cry even more but at the same time I am flooded with emotions of comfort and peace. I feel the presence of the wondrous beings.

This is how they speak to us: Out of the depth of our being they let us get messages, through our dreams, through the emotions which emerge in us, through words in a conversation that become meaningful, through sentences in a book that catch our intention, or through songs that all of a sudden come to mind.

At times I walk the familiar paths that I traveled with Prince. One morning, when my daughters were at school, I drove to our favorite wooded trail. The sun was shining, birds were singing, trees in full bloom - a magnificent day. I sat down on a rock and looked out over the lake. No one was around. I was alone with nature and my thoughts.

"You wondrous beings," I said, "help me understand why Prince had to die so soon."

I closed my eyes and let my mind become quiet and calm. Then I listened. After a long while images of

The Magic of Inner Silence

Prince appeared - how he came to our family, shy and scared but learned to trust us, how happily he played with the kids, how regally he walked at my side. Most notably, he waited for us in that dreary, sad first home in this new country and filled both homes with love.

Were these last thoughts my own thoughts? Somehow they came to my mind unexpectedly. But, yes, it is true! He had filled our home with light and love. In a very difficult time, he had held the frequency of love for us. The scales fell from my eyes.

Prince had died from cancer of the liver. The liver is the most important organ of detoxification. Prince's liver did not only detoxify material substances in his body. Prince had detoxified the depressing atmosphere in that dreary house. He let all the energies of anger, resentment and pain pass through him, thus cleansing the atmosphere for us.

All the time I thought I was the one who took care of him in this lifetime and who protected him, but it was he who protected my family. That was his life's purpose.

His life, so painful at the beginning, was destined to help us in our deepest time of need. His energies of love and loyalty gave me the courage to continue on my unusual path in America despite all difficulties. In that enlightening moment, I saw my life from a much higher perspective. The past years shone with a brilliant clarity.

The pain, however, remained.

"Why? Why? I would have preferred sorrow and pain if Prince had stayed with me, healthy and happy."

For a long while all was quiet and silent inside. No image, no emotion, no answer. Then something changed. I felt a presence, the presence of two beings. At my left side Prince was sitting. He touched me. I did not feel him with the nerves of my skin but with finer senses. I felt him unmistakably.

To my right side a male figure was standing. At first I only sensed him, then I could see him. The man was wearing a white monk's habit and sandals at his feet. He had curly brown hair, brown eyes, a kind mouth with a slim beard around his chin.

Interestingly, I had seen his eyes at times throughout my life, always when something important was to happen. Is he one of my spiritual guides? I wondered. But now it was just good to feel his presence and the presence of Prince.

Together we looked out over the lake. I received information about things I will do in my life and learned that this was the reason Prince had come into my life - to help me. As important as these revelations were, at the time I found it much more important to just sit at the lake side by side with these two loving beings and let the sun shine on me.

Kindle the Fire in Your Heart

Love is the strongest force in the universe. The more we truly love and accept ourselves, the stronger we radiate this love to all beings near and far. Then the whole world radiates this love back to us.

Bring your fingers together
and gently tap your breastbone
above the thymus,
the seat of the mystical heart.

Chant the sacred sound "AUM" out
loud or silent in your mind
(like "AAAAUUUUMMMM")
repeatedly.

Sing the tone, which feels right for you.
Do this exercise every morning
and whenever you feel lonely or sad.

The Sparrows' Innocence

What would spring in New England be without sparrows! They hop from branch to branch. They nest in bushes and trees and flutter around the house. When you open the door, you hear their small wings flapping even before you see them land on the branches. They have so much to talk about. The days are not long enough for all their stories.

There, nearby, some sparrows are sitting on the grass. They hardly move. The wind fluffs their feathers. Why do they sit there so quietly and comfortably in the sunshine instead of moving around in search of food like all the other sparrows? Now some sparrows are landing next to them.

These are a little bigger and carry food in their beaks. I conclude these must be the sparrow-parents. The young sparrow-lazybones open their beaks wide for a worm or a fly. The parents deliver, then hurry away to search and hunt, coming back again with more food.

I watch the young sparrows sitting in the bright sun. My pen rests. My thoughts are quiet. They sit there so peacefully, so contentedly, so trustingly. They don't seem to worry. They don't seem to be afraid. They sit with the innocent expectation that their needs are being met. This innocence touches me.

I wish I could feel so innocent! I wish I could feel so sheltered! Why do I long for this? Why do I not experience this for myself? Why do I seem to feel so different from the sparrows? I sit next to them in the same garden. The same wind, which ruffles their feathers, is playing with my hair. The sun shines on me as it shines on them. What is different? Why do I not feel this natural trust? What holds me back from feeling the same trust in life as the sparrows do? I do feel that they have trust. I also feel that I do not have this trust, at least not as deeply as they do.

What holds me back from sitting in the sunshine and simply enjoying it? There is restlessness; there are worries, even fear. I have duties. There are matters, which I must take care of before I can allow myself to feel carefree and secure. It feels as if I don't have the right to surrender to the present moment freely and happily.

What would happen if I could become as carefree as the sparrows? What if I sat in the sunshine trusting that everything will turn out well, knowing that the universe provides for me as it does for the sparrows?

Did I not learn that we create our reality, our life circumstances? Do I have to do things to be worthy of the riches of the universe? Is it not enough to simply accept the abundance of the universe?

The snag is not with the universe. The snag is with me. Somehow I do not feel worthy enough. It feels as if I would have to become someone else, or at least somehow different from what I am now before I am good enough, before I am perfect. Well then, are the sparrows perfect? Let me feel if this is so.

I allow my thoughts/emotions drift toward the sparrows. They are without doubt. They are simply sparrows. That's what they are one hundred percent. They are perfectly at ease with who they are. They are perfect.

I look at them with closed eyes. They shine like small round flames.

I, too, want to shine. I, too, want to be light. So I breathe in light.

That's what I have long known. That's what I have so often done. But at times I forget. Sometimes the outside world with its fears and sorrows gets louder and more important, and then I forget to breathe in light.

But now once again I breathe in light through all the pores of my body. I breathe in light and let it

The Magic of Inner Silence

shine through my entire body and through my energy fields. How good it is to feel this life energy moving through me.

Quieter and quieter I become, brighter and brighter. I hear something - a soft pounding, a persistent pounding. Is this my heartbeat? Or is this the heartbeat of Mother Earth? I caution myself, "Don't ask! Don't think! Be still. Breathe. Be light."

Then something stirs inside me. Energies shift. I become aware of an intimacy, of something that has always been there. I feel my inner energy field, my inner presence again.

Now I feel it clearly and distinctly: a knowing of being fundamentally good. I am good. Simply good, undoubtedly good. Simply a human being.

I belong here, to this time, to this space. Everything is all right. Everything is perfect. I am perfect as I am, as the sparrows are perfect as they are.

Warmed by the golden sunshine, fanned by the gentle breeze, held by our Mother Earth I am aware of myself, I know myself, I accept myself, I love myself.

Suddenly there is the sound of twigs rustling and wings fluttering. I grab our tomcat Jonathan, who has come around the corner, and hold him in my arms. The young sparrows sit in the bushes and look down on this fearsome tiger.

Jonathan snuggles in my arms, perfectly himself, simply good.

In the structure of life we all have the 'right space.' For rocks and trees this space is relatively stable. The space for animals in this structure is more fluent.

The Magic of Inner Silence

We humans determine ourselves where our space is, from breath to breath, from thought to thought. We can stay in the shadow, worrying and doubting, or we can step into the sunshine with trust.

The universe smiles at you in every blossom, in every bird song, in the sparkling of the stars.

Brigitte Novalis

You are unique.

You are precious.

You are beloved.

Epilogue

As I sit here in my back yard, writing these words, a flood of thoughts wells up in me and flows out. I sense the sunshine warming my skin and the soft wind playing with my hair. I hear birds tittering and leaves rustling.

A car drives by and connects me with streets and houses and people in my town. A plane flies high above on its way to Logan Airport and weaves a net of relations between itself and me and far away cities and people.

Children are laughing in a garden nearby. I feel the earth under my feet and know that she holds and carries me in a friendly and reliable way. I smell the scent of rosemary and thyme. Embedded in a stream of emotional intensities, I drift to new landscapes of beingness.

Small white clouds are wandering across the light blue sky high above. To me, these clouds are not any clouds. They are connected with me, with my life, with my being here. They are my clouds, but they are also your clouds and the sparrows' clouds.

Again I feel/look at the sparrows with closed eyes. Some years ago I would not have been aware of their energies but my journey into inner silence and into nature has sharpened my inner senses. Yes, they shine, the sparrows. They sit there like small round flames.

I also shine, for now I am alive again. I am at home in my body and on planet earth. I am aware of being interwoven in this net of life which stretches from me to the sparrows beside me to the Milky Way somewhere there and far beyond into eternity. Life is rich and colorful and full of surprises, every moment new.

I laugh as I write this. I laugh, simply out of pure joy. Am I always joyful? No. Am I always wise? No. But I am on my way, just as you, kind reader.

In a mysterious way I was always aware of you because I have written down my stories for you. I knew that sometime you would browse the internet for some fresh, new books and find this one. "The Magic of Inner Silence?" you would ask yourself when you see this book and take a closer look at it. "What on earth is the Magic of Inner Silence?" And thus the journey has begun for you, too.

Brigitte Novalis

About the Author

Brigitte Novalis is from Germany, but now lives with her family near Boston, Massachusetts. She works as an intuitive healer, therapist and Reiki Master.

Brigitte is also a motivational author and has written books, in both English and German, on rediscovering your joy of life, connecting with nature, and finding love.

As far back as she can remember, Brigitte has also been a devotee of fairy-tales. Since her early childhood, she has marveled at the tales of dragons, magic, princes and princesses living in faraway lands and castles.

Brigitte is now devoting part of her time to dreaming up new adventures and writing stories, which captivate children and adults alike.

Brigitte Novalis

You can connect with Brigitte online here:
brigittenovalis.com

The pictures and their artists

Brigitte Novalis

Patrick Guenette ©123RF.com

Patrick Guenette © 123RF.com

The Magic of Inner Silence

Anna Pugach © 123RF.com

Anna Pugach © 123RF.com

Denis Barbulat ©123RF.com

Anna Pugach © 123RF.com

The Magic of Inner Silence

Slobodan Zivkovic/Shutterstock.com

Valentyna Smordova © 123RF.com

Morphart Creation/Shutterstock.com

makar/Shutterstock.com

The Magic of Inner Silence

Patrick Guenette ©123RF.com

makar/Shutterstock.com

Patrick Guenette © 123RF.com

Patrick Guenette ©123RF.com

The Magic of Inner Silence

Patrick Guenette © 123RF.com

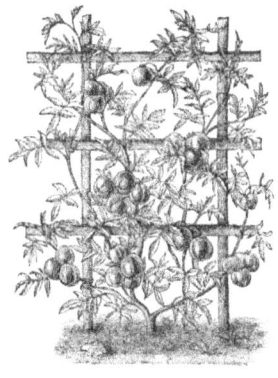

Hein Nouwens/Shutterstock.com

Brigitte Novalis

Constantina Dirica ©123RF.com

Eric Isselee © 123RF.com

The Magic of Inner Silence

tassel78 ©123RF.com

Konstantin Kozulko © 123RF.com

Victoria Levitskaya © 123RF.com

Hong Li © 123RF.com

The Magic of Inner Silence

Kav777©123RF.com

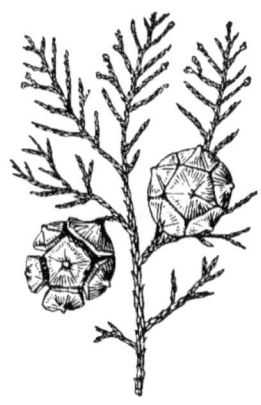

Denis Barbulat © 123RF.com

hillway ©123RF.com

Solveig/Shutterstock.com

The Magic of Inner Silence

Svetlana Corghencea © 123RF.com

Sirichai Raksue © 123RF.com

Brigitte Novalis

Volodymyr Khodaryev © 123RF.com

Patrick Guenette ©123RF.com

The Magic of Inner Silence

Patrick Guenette ©123RF.com

Nikolay Mossolaynen © 123RF.com

Konstantin Kozulko © 123RF.com

Oxana Reshetnyova © 123RF.com

The Magic of Inner Silence

PREDRAG ILIEVSKI ©123RF.com

makar/Shutterstock.com

Brigitte Novalis

Ksenia Yusupova © 123RF.com

ckchiu/Shutterstock.com

The Magic of Inner Silence

typau © 123RF.com

Susan Richey-Schmitz © 123RF.com

Brigitte Novalis

Patrick Guenette ©123RF.com

Evgeny Turaev/Shutterstock.com

The Magic of Inner Silence

Agnieszka Majchrzak/Shutterstock.com

paranormal/Shutterstsock.com

100ker/Shutterstock.com

Engin Korkmaz © 123RF.com

The Magic of Inner Silence

Engin Korkmaz © 123RF.com

Tatiana Petrova © 123RF.com

anais/Shutterstock.com

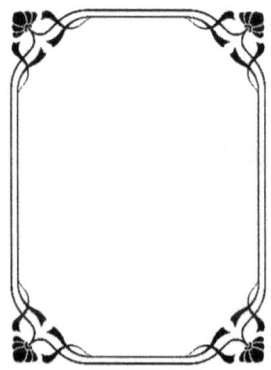

100ker/Shutterstock.com

The Magic of Inner Silence

Smileus/Shutterstock.com

www.ingramcontent.com/pod-product-compliance
Lightning Source LLC
Chambersburg PA
CBHW071704040426
42446CB00011B/1914